Cambridge Elements ☰

Elements in Money and Banking
edited by
Chao Gu
University of Missouri
Joseph Haslag
Auburn University

AF215149

MONETARY POLICY IMPLEMENTATION

Stephen Williamson
University of Western Ontario

CAMBRIDGE
UNIVERSITY PRESS

Shaftesbury Road, Cambridge CB2 8EA, United Kingdom

One Liberty Plaza, 20th Floor, New York, NY 10006, USA

477 Williamstown Road, Port Melbourne, VIC 3207, Australia

314–321, 3rd Floor, Plot 3, Splendor Forum, Jasola District Centre,
New Delhi – 110025, India

Cambridge University Press is part of Cambridge University Press & Assessment,
a department of the University of Cambridge.

We share the University's mission to contribute to society through the pursuit of
education, learning and research at the highest international levels of excellence.

www.cambridge.org
Information on this title: www.cambridge.org/9781009706834

DOI: 10.1017/9781009706810

When citing this work, please include a reference to the DOI 10.1017/9781009706810

First published 2026

A catalogue record for this publication is available from the British Library

*A Cataloging-in-Publication data record for this Element is available from the Library
of Congress*

ISBN 978-1-009-70683-4 Paperback
ISSN 2977-7585 (online)
ISSN 2977-7577 (print)

Cambridge University Press & Assessment has no responsibility for the persistence
or accuracy of URLs for external or third-party internet websites referred to in this
publication and does not guarantee that any content on such websites is, or will
remain, accurate or appropriate.

For EU product safety concerns, contact us at Calle de José Abascal, 56, 1°, 28003
Madrid, Spain, or email eugpsr@cambridge.org

Monetary Policy Implementation

Elements in Money and Banking

DOI: 10.1017/9781009706810
First published online: April 2026

Stephen Williamson
University of Western Ontario

Author for correspondence: Stephen Williamson, swilliamecon@gmail.com

Abstract: Monetary policy implementation refers to the mechanism for interbank payments, the set of administered interest rates, and the strategy for central bank actions designed to achieve an intermediate monetary policy goal – for example, a target for an overnight nominal interest rate. This Element shows the implications of the Poole model – a common framework used to articulate ideas about monetary policy implementation – for corridor and floor systems of monetary policy implementation. A general equilibrium Poole-type dynamic model is also studied, which shows where Poole-type analysis can go wrong. Given current interest in how large central bank balance sheets and floor systems matter, the Element also analyzes a general equilibrium model of quantitative easing and discusses issues with quantitative easing and monetary policy.

Keywords: implementation, monetary policy, central banking, quantitative easing, floors and corridors

ISBNs: 9781009706834 (PB), 9781009706810 (OC)
ISSNs: 2977-7585 (online), 2977-7577 (print)

Contents

1 Introduction

It is useful to structure an approach to the science of monetary policy in terms of monetary policy goals, policy rules, and implementation. We might think of aggregate economic welfare as the ultimate goal for a central bank, but typically central bankers think in terms of summary statistics – an inflation target, as in many countries of the world currently, or a dual mandate that includes an inflation target and some notion that the central bank should attempt to manage real aggregate economic activity, as in the United States. Typically though, a central bank's goals are not under its direct control, so it needs to think in terms of some intermediate target and how control of that intermediate target permits achieving the central bank's ultimate goals. A standard approach for inflation-targeting central banks is to treat a nominal interest rate on overnight credit as an intermediate target. In this context, a policy rule is a mapping from observable economic variables to a setting for the target for the overnight nominal interest rate. The science of monetary policy is then in part about how the operating characteristics of the aggregate economy depend on the choice of the monetary policy rule and, more specifically, how the monetary policy rule should be chosen to best accomplish the central bank's goals.

But, having chosen an intermediate target, the central bank's job is not done, as typically the central bank does not directly control the intermediate target variable. For example, central banks cannot, in general, dictate the overnight nominal interest rate. Implementation refers to the process by which the central bank achieves its intermediate target. This process includes the design of wholesale payments systems (the systems that comprise the infrastructure and rules governing intraday payments among financial institutions), the setting of administered interest rates – including the interest rate at which the central bank lends to private banks and the interest rate on reserves held overnight – as well as balance sheet policy and standing borrowing and lending facilities.[1]

Central bank implementation may be determined in part by the monetary policy rule. For example, the Bank of Japan was the first central bank to experiment with quantitative easing (QE) – large-scale asset purchases. Following the global financial crisis in 2008–2009, the use of QE became widespread, with the Federal Reserve System (the Fed), the Swiss National Bank, the European Central Bank, the Bank of Japan, and the Swedish central bank, among others, conducting QE operations. Under QE, central banks typically have another intermediate target in addition to an overnight nominal interest rate target:

---

[1] In the United States, the Fed has a standing reverse repo facility and a standing repo facility, which allow daily intervention on both sides of the market in repurchase agreements.

the size and composition of the central bank's balance sheet. Under QE, the balance sheet becomes sufficiently large that conventional swaps of reserves for short-maturity assets are essentially irrelevant, but swaps of reserves for long-maturity assets could matter for long bond yields.

So long as the supply of central bank reserves is sufficiently small, the central bank operates under a corridor implementation system. In such a system, intervention by the central bank in credit markets matters for the overnight nominal interest rate, which is bounded by the interest rate at which the central bank lends to private banks, on the high side, and the interest rate at which central bank reserves are remunerated, on the low side. Then, each day, the central bank's intervention policy is designed to achieve its overnight nominal interest rate target. However, with a sufficiently plentiful supply of reserve balances overnight in the banking system, the central bank operates under a floor implementation system. In this case, financial arbitrage dictates that the overnight nominal interest rate cannot deviate from the interest rate on reserves, at least in the absence of market frictions (which have actually proved to be important). So, at least in theory, targeting the overnight nominal interest rate is just a matter of setting an administered rate – the interest rate on reserve balances. Though a floor system implies that targeting the overnight interest rate can be trivial, how and what assets are purchased under QE is nontrivial.

The nature of financial markets is also important to how monetary policy implementation works. In particular, overnight credit markets, at least in part, are over-the-counter markets in which it may take time for would-be-counterparties to find each other and arrange a trade. This potentially creates issues for central bank intervention, in that the timing of interventions matter, and interest rate targeting can be imperfect.

An important element of monetary policy implementation is the design of the wholesale payments system. This is the system on which financial institutions make payments to each other during the day, and in which the central bank participates, by way of overnight lending and borrowing. As well, the facilities of the central bank dovetail with the wholesale payments system in that end-of-day clearing and settlement typically involves central bank participation. That is, payments system participants who are indebted at the end of the day borrow from the central bank, and participants in a positive net credit position hold central bank reserves overnight. There are alternative mechanisms for intraday wholesale payments systems, the two main mechanisms being real-time gross settlement, where debts are settled intraday in reserve balances in real time, and net settlement systems, where debt positions evolve over the day as payments are made and then the participant's net position is settled at the end of the day. In practice, wholesale payments systems can be hybrids, including elements of real-time gross settlement and netting. Alternative systems have different implications for risk bearing and incentives, as do the rules for securing within-day credit and for limiting the use of within-day credit.

In this Element, we first consider a baseline model of monetary policy implementation, the Poole (1968) model, which is the basis for much work on implementation. We show how the model works, in a modern context, show its implications for floor versus corridor systems, and for reserve tiering and voluntary reserve targeting, and discuss its limitations.

The Poole model neglects the relationship between retail and wholesale payments, dynamics, and secured overnight credit. So, it seemed useful to explore a model that goes some way toward correcting these problems. This second model, introduced in this Element, can be used to evaluate the relative efficiency of corridor and floor systems of monetary policy implementation. We find that a floor system of monetary policy implementation can be optimal in this model but for reasons different from the ones typically given by central bankers in support of floor systems.

As well, to consider other issues in monetary policy implementation under floor and corridor systems or large-versus small-balance-sheet central banking, we construct a general equilibrium model of QE, based on Williamson (2016). In the model, QE can have the effect of flattening the yield curve, in line with what proponents of QE allege. However, the model also tells us that QE is essentially government debt management conducted by the central bank and that it can have general equilibrium effects that are apparently not part of the QE playbook.

Finally, we discuss an alternative notion of what may lie at the heart of the effects of QE, if there are any significant effects at all. The empirical evidence on QE is discussed, as well as some potential threats to central bank independence that can arise as the result of aggressive QE operations by central banks.

2 Baseline Implementation Theory: The Poole Model

The Poole 1968 model, though more than fifty years old, remains the most common tool used by central bankers in the United States and elsewhere for analyzing monetary policy implementation. Using the model, we can derive an individual bank's demand for reserve balances and then aggregate to determine the market demand for reserves. This then allows us to analyze the effects of central bank intervention and corridor versus floor systems.

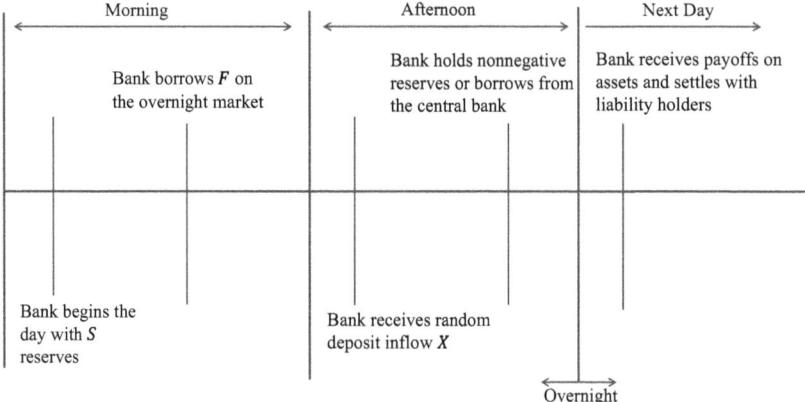

Figure 1 Timeline for the individual bank.

2.1 Bank Behavior

The model constructed here contains the essential features of the Poole (1968) model, but there are differences in detail and emphasis. Poole considered a model with reserve requirements and no interest on reserves, and he did not consider the implications of his model for floor systems of monetary policy implementation. This conformed to the institutional setup of 1968 in the United States, but to fit typical current central banking arrangements, particularly those in the United States, we consider a model with no reserve requirements and interest on reserves, and the analysis of floor systems will be important.

Start with an individual bank, assumed to be a price taker in the overnight credit market, which Poole interpreted to be the federal funds market. There is a single period, with two subperiods we will denote the morning and afternoon. The individual bank's timeline is depicted in Figure 1. Let R^d, R^f, R^b, and R^s denote, respectively, the interest rate on discount window loans from the central bank, the overnight interest rate (the fed funds rate), the interest rate on the bank's deposits, and the interest rate on reserves held with the central bank. At the beginning of the day, the bank has S units of reserves on hand. For simplicity, assume that reserves are the bank's only asset and that the bank begins the day with zero net worth.[2] The bank's only liabilities are deposits, so if D denotes the bank's deposits, then $D = S$ at the beginning of the day. In the morning, the bank makes a decision concerning borrowing, F, on the overnight market. In the overnight market, reserves are exchanged for overnight IOUs,

---

[2] If we assumed that the bank holds some other illiquid assets that cannot be traded during the day, this would make no difference for our analysis.

and these IOUs are settled at the beginning of the next day. Since reserves cannot be negative, the bank faces the constraint

$$S + F \geq 0. \tag{1}$$

That is, the overnight market consists of exchanges of reserve balances for overnight IOUs, so equation (1) states that the bank can lend no more reserves than what it has at the beginning of the day. Here, if $F > 0$ the bank is a borrower on the overnight market, and if $F < 0$ it is a lender.

Then, in the afternoon, after the overnight market has closed, the bank experiences a random deposit inflow, which could be negative. Let X denote the deposit inflow, which is distributed according to the probability distribution function $G(X)$. Assume that $G(X)$ is continuous and differentiable on the support for the distribution, which is $[\underline{X}, \bar{X}]$. Assume $\underline{X} < 0$ and $\bar{X} > 0$.

This model is simple, which is certainly a virtue. But, in terms of what might or should be of interest, it may omit some important features. For example, in the Introduction we discussed how the mechanism by which daily wholesale payments are conducted could be important for monetary policy implementation. But in the basic Poole model, the individual bank makes no payments during the day. Random deposit outflows are certainly part of what happens in practice as the result of underlying retail payments driving interbank payments, but there is not enough detail to help the researcher analyze problems in wholesale payments system design and monetary policy.

We will now proceed to determine the individual bank's behavior in this environment. If

$$S + F + X \leq 0, \tag{2}$$

then the bank is short of reserves at the end of the day, and must borrow $-(S + F + X)$ from the discount window overnight to bring reserve balances up to zero. The bank's deposits at the end of the day will be $S + X$, independent of F, so the bank's profits in this case are

$$\pi(F, X) = -F(1 + R^f) + (S + F + X)(1 + R^d) - (S + X)(1 + R^b). \tag{3}$$

Alternatively, if

$$S + F + X \geq 0, \tag{4}$$

then the bank holds positive reserves at the end of the day, and the bank's profits are given by

$$\pi(F, X) = -F(1 + R^f) + (S + F + X)(1 + R^s) - (S + X)(1 + R^b). \tag{5}$$

The bank is assumed to be risk neutral, and maximizes $H(F) = E[\pi(F, X)]$. First, from (3) and (5), if $F \epsilon [-S, -S - \underline{X}]$ then

$$H(F) = (R^b - R^d) \int_{\underline{X}}^{-S-F} G(X)dX + F(R^s - R^f)$$

$$+ S(R^s - R^b) + (R^b - R^s) \int_{-S-F}^{\bar{X}} G(X)dX. \tag{6}$$

And, if $F \geq -S - \underline{X}$, then from (5), we get

$$H(F) = F(R^s - R^f) + S(R^s - R^b) + (R^s - R^b) \int_{\underline{X}}^{\bar{X}} X dG(X). \tag{7}$$

So, from (6) and (7), $H(F)$ is continuously differentiable for $F \geq -S$, with

$$H'(F) = (R^d - R^s)G(-S - F) + R^s - R^f, \tag{8}$$

for $F \epsilon [-S, -S - \underline{X}]$ and

$$H'(F) = R^s - R^f, \tag{9}$$

for $F \geq -S - \underline{X}$. As well,

$$H''(F) = -(R^d - R^s)g(-S - F), \tag{10}$$

for $F \epsilon [-S, -S - \underline{X}]$ and

$$H''(F) = 0, \tag{11}$$

for $F \geq -S - \underline{X}$.

Assume that the central bank sets R^d and R^s so that $R^d > R^s$. Then, if $R^f \geq R^d G(0) + R^s [1 - G(0)]$, from (8) and (9), we have $H'(F) \leq 0$ for $F \geq -S$, so in this case the bank chooses

$$F = -S.$$

If $R^s < R^f < R^d G(0) + R^s [1 - G(0)]$, then from (8), (9), (10), and (11), we obtain an interior solution, where the inverted demand curve for the firm, determined by setting $H'(F) = 0$ in (8), is

$$R^f = R^d G(-S - F) + R^s [1 - G(-S - F)]. \tag{12}$$

Finally, from (8) and (9), if $R^f = R^s$, then

$$F \geq -S - \underline{X}, \tag{13}$$

and if $R^f < R^s$, then

$$F = \infty.$$

The bank's demand curve for overnight loans is then as depicted in Figure 2. If the interest rate in the overnight market were greater than or equal to the discount rate, then it would be profitable for the bank to lend as much as possible

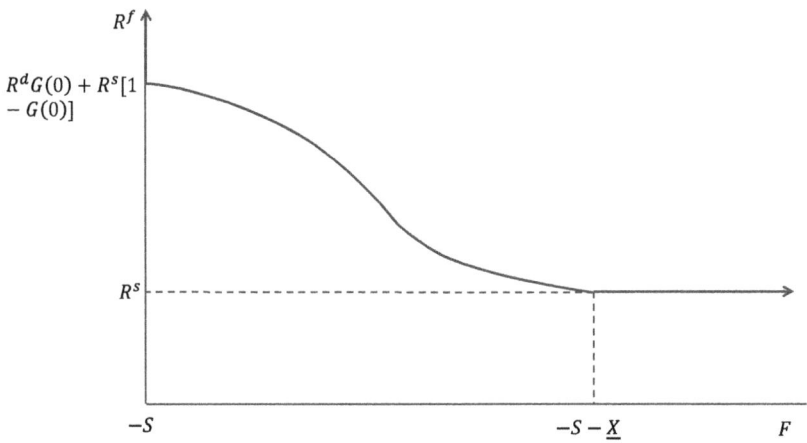

Figure 2 Individual bank's demand for overnight loans as a function of the overnight interest rate.

in the overnight market and finance this by borrowing from the discount window. Also, in the event that the overnight interest rate is less than the interest rate on reserves, it is profitable for the bank to borrow an infinite amount on the overnight market and hold the proceeds as overnight reserves. If the overnight interest rate is equal to the interest rate on reserves, then the bank wants to borrow on the overnight market, at least to the point where it will always have nonnegative reserves overnight, and beyond that it is indifferent about the quantity of reserves it holds. In the event that the overnight rate falls between the interest rate on reserves and the discount rate, equation (12) states that the bank will borrow on the overnight market up to the point where the cost of overnight borrowing is equal to the expected value of the net benefit from borrowing.

Note that, in making decisions about overnight borrowing, the bank will be trading off the marginal costs of two types of ex post errors. First, the bank could borrow too little on the overnight market and then have to borrow at a higher interest rate from the central bank at the discount window. Second, the bank could borrow too much, and the interest rate at which it borrows is then greater than the payoff it receives from holding reserves overnight.

2.2 Market Equilibrium and Monetary Policy Implementation

Having derived an individual bank's demand for overnight reserves, we can in principle aggregate across banks to determine the market demand for reserves. In aggregating, of course, we would have to make assumptions about the nature of heterogeneity across banks. To get some idea the implications of the model for what we should observe in the overnight market, suppose that there is a

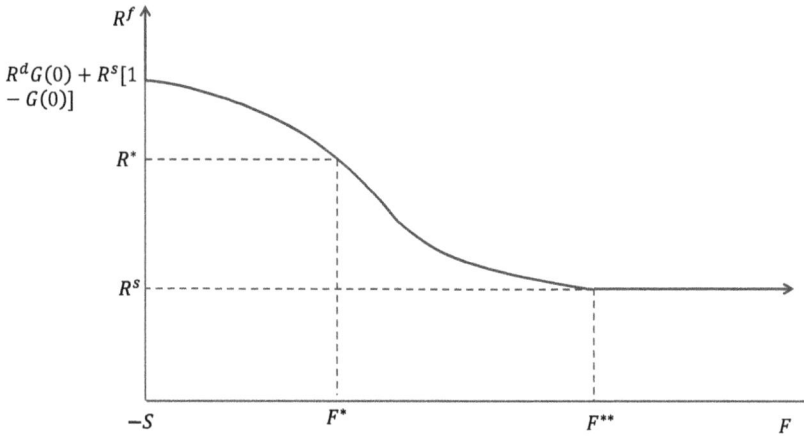

Figure 3 Market demand for overnight loans as a function of the overnight interest rate.

continuum of banks with unit mass, and they are all identical, starting the day with the same quantity of reserve balances and facing the same distribution function for deposit inflows. For this distribution function to be consistent with flows in the aggregate (in that one bank's deposit inflow is another bank's outflow), we require that $E[X] = 0$.

In this case, the market demand for overnight loans is identical to the individual bank's demand in Figure 2. Then, in a corridor system, where the central bank wants to target $R^f = R^*$, with $R^s < R^* < R^d$, the supply of overnight loans by the central bank would be F^* in Figure 3, which achieves the target R^* for the overnight interest rate. Note that implicit in this corridor system is some degree of intervention through the discount window. Total discount window lending must equal

$$D^* = \int_{\underline{X}}^{-S-F^*} (-S - F^* - X)dG(X) = \int_{\underline{X}}^{-S-F^*} G(X)dX.$$

So, this implies that the larger is F^*, or the smaller is the target interest rate, R^*, the less intervention is required through the discount window.

In a floor system, there is a critical level of lending F^{**} that central bank intervention in the overnight market must exceed, as shown in Figure 3. In a floor system, the overnight rate is $R^f = R^s$ so, by arbitrage, the central bank need only set the interest rate on reserves administratively and then lend at least F^{**} in the overnight market. Under a floor system, there is no discount window lending. In the model, it appears that the floor system always involves intervention by the central bank. But note that this is a static model, and in practice the floor system would imply that S, reserve balances held at the beginning of the day, is high. That is, from (13), if $S \geq -\underline{X}$, then the overnight market clears at $R^f = R^s$ with $F = 0$, and there is no need for intervention by the central bank.

If we think in particular about the organization of US intervention in overnight markets, this setup might not seem to fit. While the Fed was running a corridor system, in the period before the global financial crisis, the Federal Open Market Committee (FOMC) targeted the federal funds rate but intervened in the repo market. While these two markets are intertwined, the repo market is different from the fed funds market, as the repo market has more participants and more activity, the repo market is a market in secured credit while the fed funds market is unsecured, and participation in the fed funds market requires that a financial institution has a reserve account with the Fed. Thus, the Poole model is typically analyzed as a market in reserves, where the market demand for reserves is initial reserves plus total net demand for loans on the overnight market, and reserves supplied by the central bank in the overnight market is equal to central bank lending (and note that the central bank can potentially supply negative reserves by borrowing on the overnight market). This means that the basic Poole model sweeps some issues under the rug, relating to secured and unsecured overnight markets, as we will discuss in what follows.

The model gives predictions about total overnight reserves and the distribution of overnight reserves across banks. Assume, as in the analysis for an individual bank, that banks have identical beginning-of-day reserves and face the same distribution of deposit inflows. First, in a corridor system, given an overnight interest rate target $R^f = R^*$, supported by central bank lending in the overnight market F^* and discount window lending D^*, a fraction $G(-S - F^*)$ of banks borrows from the discount window and holds zero reserve balances overnight. The remaining fraction of banks, $1 - G(-S - F^*)$, holds reserves in excess of zero, with the distribution of reserves across these banks determined by the distribution of X, conditional on $X \geq -S - F^*$. In the aggregate, total reserves held overnight is given by

$$Y = \int_{-S-F^*}^{\bar{X}} (S + F^* + X)\, dG(X) = S + F^* + \bar{X} - \int_{-S-F^*}^{\bar{X}} G(X)\,dX.$$

So,

$$\frac{\partial Y}{\partial F^*} = 1 - G(-S - F^*).$$

Therefore, a decline in the target overnight interest rate, which in turn implies an increase in F^*, increases overnight reserves, but less than one-for-one with the increase in reserves injected in the overnight market, as discount window lending declines.

Under a floor system, there is no discount window lending, and an individual bank holds overnight reserves $S + F^* + X$, so the distribution of reserves across banks is just the distribution $G(X)$ shifted to the right by $S + F^*$. And, since $E[X] = 0$, total reserves are equal to $S + F^*$.

Another approach to monetary policy implementation is for the central bank to borrow S at the interest rate R^d in the overnight market. This then implies that the market-clearing overnight interest rate is R^d. Then, any bank with $X < 0$ borrows at the discount window at the end of the day, and all banks hold zero reserves overnight. As with a floor system, the overnight interest rate is determined by an interest rate administered by the central bank.

2.3 Reserve Tiering and Voluntary Reserve Targets

Reserve tiering was first practiced in regimes with negative interest rates on bank reserves, including the Euro area, Japan, and Switzerland. Potentially, negative nominal interest rates squeeze bank profits, as it may not be profit-maximizing for banks to pass on negative interest rates to bank depositors. This is because zero-interest currency always exists as an alternative to bank deposits for small depositors. Currency may be a less convenient alternative, but the lower are negative interest rates, the more attractive currency becomes for bank depositors, and the more depositors will flee to currency from bank deposits. Negative interest rates may then result in disintermediation and could impair the allocation of credit.

A potential solution for this problem, implemented in practice, is for the central bank to remunerate reserves at a higher rate below some threshold (which could be bank-specific) and at the desired negative rate above the threshold. This increases bank profits, but in principle the marginal interest rate on reserve balances should determine the overnight interest rate.

To see how this works, let T denote the threshold for reserve tiering. So, since reserves at the end of the day comprise reserves at the beginning of the day, plus borrowing on the overnight market, plus the deposit inflow, or $S + F + X$, interest is paid at the rate R^d if $S + F + X < 0$ (reserves are topped up to zero with a discount window loan), R_1^s if $0 \leq S + F + X \leq T$, and interest is paid at the rate R_2^s if $S + F + X > T$, where $T > 0$. Then, follow the same approach as in the baseline case, in deriving expected profits for the bank as a function $H(F)$. Then, expected profits for an individual bank, if $F \epsilon [-S, -S - \underline{X}]$, are given by

$$H(F) = -FR^f - SR^b + -R^b E[X]$$

$$+ R_2^s(F + S + \bar{X}) + (R_1^s - R_2^s)T - R^d \int_{\underline{X}}^{-S-F} G(X)dX$$

$$- R_1^s \int_{-S-F}^{T-S-F} G(X)dX - R_2^s \int_{T-S-F}^{\bar{X}} G(X)dX.$$

And, if $F\epsilon[-S - \underline{X}, -S - \underline{X} + T]$,

$$H(F) = -FR^f - SR^b - E[X]R^b - R_1^s \int_{\underline{X}}^{T-S-F} G(X)dX$$

$$+ (F + S)R_2^s + T(R_1^s - R_2^s) - R_2^s \int_{T-S-F}^{\bar{X}} G(X)dX.$$

Finally, if $F \geq -S - \underline{X} + T$, then

$$H(F) = -FR^f - SR^b - E[X]R^b + T(R_1^s - R_2^s)$$

$$+ (F + S)R_2^s + R_2^s \bar{X} - R_2^s \int_{\underline{X}}^{\bar{X}} G(X)dX.$$

Then, for $F\epsilon[-S, -S - \underline{X}]$, we get

$$H'(F) = -R^f + R^d G(-S - F) + R_1^s [G(T - S - F) - G(-S - F)]$$

$$+ R_2^s [1 - G(T - S - F)]$$

and, for $F\epsilon[-S - \underline{X}, -S - \underline{X} + T]$,

$$H'(F) = -R^f + R_1^s G(T - S - F) + R_2^s [1 - G(T - S - F)]. \tag{14}$$

And, finally, for $F \geq -S - \underline{X} + T$,

$$H'(F) = -R^f + R_2^s.$$

But, if we used the standard remuneration scheme, with interest rate R_2^s on all positive reserve balances, then for $F\epsilon[-S, -S - \underline{X}]$,

$$H'(F) = -R^f + R^d G(-S - F) + R_2^s [1 - G(-S - F)],$$

and if $F \geq -S - \underline{X}$, then

$$H'(F) = -R^f + R_2^s.$$

Then, the difference between derivatives in the tiered case and the standard case is, if $F\epsilon[-S, -S - \underline{X}]$,

$$\Delta = (R_1^s - R_2^s)[G(T - S - F) - G(-S - F)] > 0,$$

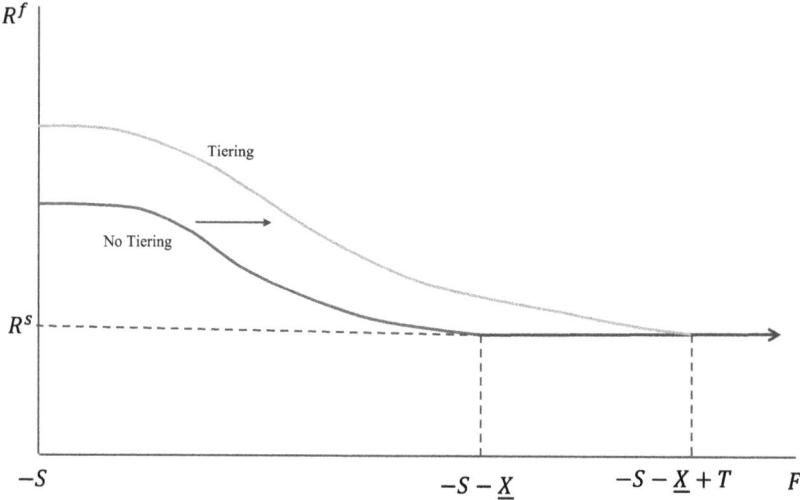

Figure 4 With reserve tiering, the individual bank's demand for overnight loans shifts to the right.

if $F \in [-S - \underline{X}, -S - \underline{X} + T]$,

$$\Delta = \left(R_1^s - R_2^s\right) G(T - S - F),$$

and if $F \geq -S - \underline{X} + T$,

$$\Delta = 0.$$

So, as depicted in Figure 4, an individual bank's demand for reserves shifts to the right with reserve tiering, and the shift is larger, the larger is the differential between the inframarginal interest rate on reserves and the marginal interest rate. This implies that, in a corridor system with tiering, there must be a larger quantity of reserves in the system for a given target overnight interest rate than without tiering. Also, with a tiered floor system, the threshold quantity of reserves required to make the floor system work is higher than without tiering. Thus, a larger central bank balance sheet is in general required to support a system of tiered reserves, and this may be undesirable.

Typically, reserve tiering has been used as an element of a floor system in circumstances where the overnight nominal interest rate target is negative, with the central bank aiming to limit the squeeze on private bank profits. But there are instances where reserve tiering is used in an environment with positive nominal interest rates. For example, since late 2022, the Swiss National Bank has paid positive interest on reserve balances up to some threshold and zero interest on reserves held above the threshold. As discussed in Swiss National Bank (2023), each bank is assigned an individual-specific threshold, and the goal is to encourage banks to shed reserves held above the threshold. That is, this arrangement encourages exchange on the overnight market, with intervention by the central bank taking place so that the market clears at the interest rate at which reserves below the threshold are remunerated.

To see how this works in the Poole model, the overnight rate is targeted at $R^f = R_1^s$, and so the quantity of lending by the central bank needs to be in the range $F \epsilon [-S - \underline{X}, -S - \underline{X} + T]$. Then, from (14), for $R^f = R_1^s$, we need

$$T - S - F = \bar{X},$$

so

$$F = -S - \bar{X} + T.$$

Then, in this world where banks are identical, with a large central bank balance sheet we take S to be large. Then, as long as T is not too large, we can have $F < 0$ in equilibrium, so the private banks are lenders on the overnight market. In practice, the central bank can run a reverse repo facility similar to the one in place in the United States, which serves to withdraw sufficient reserves from the banking system so that the overnight market clears at $R^f = R_1^s$.

Reserve tiering in the context of negative nominal interest rates is discussed in Berentsen et al. (2023), while reserve tiering in Switzerland is addressed in Fuhrer et al. (2021). Voluntary reserve targeting has been studied by Baughman and Carapella (2022, in press).

2.4 Discussion

The Poole model is simple, and simplicity is a virtue, but there are features of overnight markets neglected in the model that may be important. We will first discuss what is neglected in the Poole model. Then, in the next section, we discuss attempts in the literature to address these issues.

1. The model is static, and it would be desirable to include dynamic elements in the model so as to determine the evolution over time in the distribution of reserve balances. As is, the initial distribution of reserve balances is critical for the results, but this initial distribution is exogenous. Further, anticipation of events in the following day, and further in the future, should matter for bank behavior.

2. The overnight market is assumed to be competitive, but in practice trade in overnight credit markets occurs either over-the-counter or through third parties. Poole attempted to finesse this issue through a timing assumption, whereby there is an end-of-period shock that occurs after the overnight market closes. In practice, failure to trade may be due to a market participant

looking for a counterparty late in the trading day and failing to find one. But market participants in practice have some choice about when they want to trade during the day, and there may be issues with delay in trading, resulting in inefficiencies due to market congestion. A more detailed approach is needed to address issues related to this.

3. The model neglects secured overnight credit – all banks are assumed to be participating in an unsecured credit market, akin to the fed funds market. But the secured market – the repo market – is large relative to the fed funds market in the United States, and the repo market is the venue in which the Fed intervenes. There are important issues to do with market timing and the supply of collateral that are potentially important for how monetary policy works.

4. The details of the wholesale payments system are neglected, as mentioned, and we might like to understand how retail payments and wholesale payments are integrated and the implications for monetary policy implementation. The rules under which the payments system works are critical. For example, intraday lending by the central bank and rules concerning collateral and intraday credit matter for monetary policy implementation and for systemic risk.

2.5 Related Research

Some extensions of Poole's framework use developments in search and matching theory to structure the overnight market as an over-the-counter market. For example, Afonso and Lagos (2015a, 2015b) study fed funds market trade in continuous time over a day and derive implications for the distribution of reserve balances across banks. As well, Afonso et al. (2019) considers a search model which shares features with Poole (1968) but incorporates some key institutional features relating to the floor system in operation in the United States since late 2008.

Some authors have done empirical work which aims in part to determine the relevant empirical threshold for aggregate reserves that induces the transition to a floor system. Work in this vein includes Lagos and Navarro (2023) and Afonso et al. (2024). The latter paper also serves to characterize an intermediate range for reserves as "ample," whereas the basic Poole model has essentially two regions – abundant, characterized by aggregate reserves above some threshold, and scarce, characterized by reserves below this threshold.

Ennis and Keister (2008) is a nice summary of monetary policy implementation in a Poole-type framework, while Berentsen and Monnet (2008) contains a model of channel system implementation. Also, Ennis and Weinberg (2013) studies the issue of stigma at the Federal Reserve discount window, while Armenter and Lester (2017) addresses how monetary implementation works with a large-balance-sheet central bank.

Issues related to intraday wholesale payments and congestion are studied by Bech and Garratt (2003), for example. And Williamson (2024) considers a framework where retail payments, wholesale payments, central bank intervention, and safe asset allocation are interrelated.

2.6 A Dynamic General Equilibrium Poole-Type Model with Secured Overnight Credit

We will now consider a model that addresses some of the issues in Section 2.4. In particular, we introduce a simple model that allows for dynamics, the integration of retail and wholesale payments, and secured overnight credit. This model is in one sense new, relative to much of the implementation literature, but familiar to monetary economists who understand cash-in-advance (e.g. Lucas 1980) constructs.

The model takes a common approach to simplifying the analysis of financial relationships in embedding banking relationships within households. The "big household" approach was followed by Lucas (1990), Shi (1997), and Gertler and Kiyotaki (2011), for example. The model consists of identical households that trade using credit (interpreted as deposit claims on banks), with debts settled with reserve balances, in a type of gross settlement wholesale payments system. The fact that the model is micro-founded allows us to make welfare statements. In particular, we can evaluate the relative efficiency of floor and corridor systems of monetary policy implementation, in a way that cannot be done in a Poole-type model.

We find conditions under which the size of the central bank's corridor – the margin between the overnight interest rate target and the interest rate on reserves – matters for the equilibrium allocation of resources and for welfare. Also, we show that a floor system, under which the central bank's corridor is zero, is optimal. But we obtain this result because a floor system is most efficient, given constraints faced by the central bank, and not for the typical reasons given by central bankers.

2.6.1 The Model

There is a continuum of identical households with unit mass, each of which maximizes

$$\sum_{t=0}^{\infty} \beta^t \left[u(c_t) - v(n_t) \right],$$ (15)

where $0 < \beta < 1$, $u(\cdot)$ is strictly increasing, strictly concave, and twice continuously differentiable, c_t denotes the household's consumption, $v(\cdot)$ is strictly increasing, strictly convex, and twice continuously differentiable, and n_t denotes the household's labor supply. Assume that $u'(0) = \infty$, $v'(0) = 0$, and that $v'(h) = \infty$ for some $h > 0$. A household consists of three members: a buyer, a seller, and a bank.

A period is interpreted as a day. Timing within a period works as follows. First, households trade in an asset market, with the household facing the asset market constraint

$$c_t + b_t - f_t \leq (1 + R^s_{t-1})s_{t-1} + (1 + R^b_{t-1})b_{t-1} - (1 + R^f_{t-1})f_{t-1}$$
$$- (1 + R^d_{t-1})d_{t-1} + \tau_t \tag{16}$$

The right-hand side of (16) denotes the household's wealth at the beginning of the day, where s_{t-1}, b_{t-1}, f_{t-1}, and d_{t-1} denote, respectively, reserve balances, one-period government debt, overnight loans, and discount window loans carried forward from period $t - 1$ into period t. As well, R^s_{t-1}, R^b_{t-1}, R^f_{t-1}, R^d_{t-1}, denote the real interest rates on reserve balances, one-period government debt, overnight loans, and discount window loans, determined in period $t-1$. A lump-sum transfer received by the household (each household receives the same transfer) from the government is denoted τ_t. There is no currency in the model, and all quantities and prices are specified in units of the numeraire, which is the current consumption good. Interest rates are rates of return in terms of future consumption relative to current consumption.

On the left-hand side of equation (16), the household must finance current consumption c_t and acquisitions of newly issued government debt b_t from overnight loans l_t and beginning-of-period wealth. In the model, we have abstracted from the relationship between depositors and banks and have embedded that in the household. But adding the details of deposit taking and interbank settlement should not change the analysis in any important way. Effectively, equation (16) embodies a type of real-time gross settlement system for the settlement of interbank debts. That is, in order to finance consumption (which would imply an interbank debt that needs to be settled), the household needs to either carry forward reserve balances from the previous period or borrow reserves on the overnight market.

Next, after the asset market closes, the buyer in the household goes to the goods market to purchase goods from other households. A household is assumed to be unable to consume its own output. Goods are purchased with claims to reserve balances in the settlement phase, which follows the closing of the goods market. Also, after the asset market closes, the seller in the household goes to the goods market, produces, and exchanges goods for claims on reserve balances in the settlement phase. One unit of labor input by the seller in the household produces one unit of perishable consumption goods. So, by embedding the bank within the household, we have eliminated some details concerning the relationship between consumers and banks, and how banks conduct interbank transactions. We could model the details – depositors exchange bank deposits (claims on banks) for goods, which generates interbank debts, which in turn are settled with reserve balances – but that would not change the analysis in any important ways (if at all).

A key friction in the model – in typical cash-in-advance fashion – is that incoming payments from other households cannot finance current consumption. That is, incoming payments arrive too late to offset outgoing payments by the household. The household must satisfy its budget constraint each period, or

$$c_t + b_t - f_t + s_t - d_t = n_t + (1 + R_{t-1}^s)s_{t-1} + (1 + R_{t-1}^b)b_{t-1}$$
$$- (1 + R_{t-1}^f) f_{t-1} - (1 + R_{t-1}^d)d_{t-1} + \tau_t. \qquad (17)$$

We assume that household debts must be secured, where government debt and reserves serve as collateral. But incoming payments from other households cannot be pledged as collateral, so we write the collateral constraint for the household as

$$(1 + R_t^s)s_t + (1 + R_t^b)b_t - (1 + R_t^f) f_t - (1 + R_t^d)d_t \geq (1 + R_t^s)n_t. \qquad (18)$$

That is, the household weakly prefers to keep the payoffs on its collateral and pay its debts at the beginning of the next day, rather than absconding with incoming payments during the current day. Note in (18) that we assume that (16) holds with equality (which ignores equilibria where (16) does not bind and holds as a strict inequality).

Throughout, we will focus on symmetric equilibria in which all households make the same choices. This implies that l_t is borrowing by each household from the government in the overnight market and is also lending by the government. So, we can write the government's budget constraints as

$$s_0 + b_0 = \tau_0, \qquad (19)$$
$$s_t + b_t - f_t + (1 + R_{t-1}^f) f_{t-1} + (1 + R_{t-1}^d)d_{t-1}$$
$$= (1 + R_{t-1}^s)s_{t-1} + (1 + R_{t-1}^b)b_{t-1} + \tau_t, \qquad (20)$$

for $t = 1, 2, 3, \ldots, \infty$. So, in the initial period, the government issues reserves and bonds to finance a transfer to households, and in each succeeding period, new issues of reserves, government bonds, and the interest and principal on overnight loans and overnight discount window loans finances the interest and principal on overnight reserve balances, and the interest and principal on government debt, plus the transfer to households.

2.6.2 Household Maximization

The household chooses $\{s_t, b_t, f_t, d_t, c_t, n_t\}_{t=0}^{\infty}$ to maximize (15) subject to the constraints (16), (17), and (18). Let λ_t^1, λ_t^2, and μ_t denote, respectively, the multipliers associated with constraints (16), (18), and (17). Assume that the household faces interest rates satisfying

$$R_t^s \leq R_t^f < R_t^d, \tag{21}$$

and we will determine in what follows the central bank intervention required to support this interest rate configuration.

First, note that given (21), the household will choose $d_t = 0$, as it is cheaper to borrow on the overnight market than at the discount window. Note that borrowing at the discount window at a penalty rate occurs in the Poole model because of an unanticipated shock to net payment flows after overnight lending and borrowing occurs. But our model has perfect certainty, so there can be no borrowing at the penalty rate from the discount window.

From the household's problem, the following must hold in equilibrium:

$$-\mu_t + (1 + R_t^s)\lambda_t^2 + \beta(1 + R_t^s)\left(\lambda_{t+1}^1 + \mu_{t+1}\right) = 0, \tag{22}$$

$$-\lambda_t^1 - \mu_t + (1 + R_t^b)\lambda_t^2 + \beta(1 + R_t^b)\left(\lambda_{t+1}^1 + \mu_{t+1}\right) = 0, \tag{23}$$

$$\lambda_t^1 + \mu_t - (1 + R_t^f)\lambda_t^2 - \beta(1 + R_t^f)\left(\lambda_{t+1}^1 + \mu_{t+1}\right) = 0, \tag{24}$$

$$u'(c_t) - \lambda_t^1 - \mu_t = 0, \tag{25}$$

$$-v'(n_t) + \mu_t - (1 + R_t^s)\lambda_t^2 = 0. \tag{26}$$

Solving out for the multipliers in (22)–(26), we obtain

$$R_t^b = R_t^f, \tag{27}$$

$$-v'(n_t) + \beta(1 + R_t^s)u'(c_{t+1}) = 0. \tag{28}$$

So, from (27), the interest rates on overnight credit and government debt must be identical in equilibrium, by arbitrage, in that lending overnight and acquiring government debt imply payoffs in the same circumstances and relax the household's collateral constraint in the same way. As well, (22)–(26) imply

$$\lambda_t^1 = \frac{(R_t^f - R_t^s)u'(c_t)}{(1 + R_t^f)}, \tag{29}$$

$$\lambda_t^2 = \frac{u'(c_t)}{1 + R_t^f} - \beta u'(c_{t+1}), \tag{30}$$

and these two conditions will allow us to check for nonnegativity of the multipliers associated with the asset market and collateral constraints.

2.6.3 Equilibrium

Consider stationary and symmetric equilibria, where all variables are constant forever, and all households make the same choices. So we can drop time subscripts, and in equilibrium,

$$c = n. \tag{31}$$

Further, assume that the fiscal authority holds consolidated government debt constant, so in general

$$s + b - f = \bar{b}. \tag{32}$$

So, each period the fiscal authority issues $\bar{b}$ units of government debt, and the central bank issues s reserves to purchase government debt and to fund loans f overnight, with b the quantity of government debt left in the private sector. Therefore, s is the size of the central bank's balance sheet. The asset market constraint (16) holds with equality if $\lambda_t^1 > 0$, but confine attention to the case where (16) holds with equality if $\lambda_t^1 = 0$. So, from (16) and the government budget constraints (19) and (20),

$$c = s, \tag{33}$$

and from the collateral constraint, (18), which we assume binds (and it will bind given sufficiently small $\bar{b}$), (27), and (31)–(33),

$$c = \bar{b}. \tag{34}$$

So, (33) and (34) imply that $s = \bar{b}$, that is the size of the central bank's balance sheet is not a monetary policy choice but is dictated by fiscal policy. This result is in part determined by our assumptions about timing – basically when incoming payments are credited in relation to when the overnight credit market closes. So, we do not want to take this result too seriously.

This version of the model may not be equipped to address balance sheet policy, but we can analyze how the choice of the interest rates – the overnight interest rate target R^f and the interest rate on reserves R^s – affects variables in equilibrium. First, note that R^f and R^s cannot be chosen arbitrarily. In fact, from (24) and (34), we can solve for R^s in equilibrium, obtaining

$$R^s = \frac{v'\left(\bar{b}\right)}{\beta u'\left(\bar{b}\right)} - 1. \tag{35}$$

Then, from (29), (30), and (35), R^f must be chosen to satisfy

$$\frac{v'\left(\bar{b}\right)}{\beta u'\left(\bar{b}\right)} - 1 \le R^f \le \frac{1}{\beta} - 1. \tag{36}$$

But otherwise the choice of R^f is arbitrary, that is the size of the corridor does not matter for the equilibrium allocation but it affects whether the asset market constraint and the collateral constraint bind, from (29) and (30). In particular, it is necessary for this type of equilibrium to exist that

$$\bar{b} < c^*, \tag{37}$$

where c^* is the efficient quantity of consumption, satisfying

$$u'(c^*) - v'(c^*) = 0.$$

Here, (37) is the case where safe assets are in short supply, in that the net quantity of safe assets is insufficient to support efficiency. From (29) and (30), any setting for R^f satisfying (36) implies that either the asset market constraint, the collateral constraint, or both bind in equilibrium. But, in an equilibrium where

$$\bar{b} \ge c^*,$$

then

$$c = n = c^*,$$

and

$$R^f = R^s = \frac{1}{\beta} - 1.$$

So, if safe assets are plentiful, the equilibrium allocation is efficient, all interest rates are equal to the rate of time preference (there are no liquidity premia associated with government debt or bank reserves), and the asset market and collateral constraints do not bind.

2.6.4 Limited Payoff from Absconding

So far, this model is essentially just a sketch of a theory of secured overnight markets and monetary policy implementation, and our analysis shows that we need other details to address monetary policy implementation issues in a serious way. One simple extension is to limit the payoff the household receives from absconding, as is typical in the literature on limited commitment.

We will proceed to alter the model, first by replacing the collateral constraint (18) with

$$(1 + R_t^s)s_t + (1 + R_t^b)b_t - (1 + R_t^f)f_t - (1 + R_t^d)d_t \ge \gamma(1 + R_t^s)n_t. \tag{38}$$

In (38), γ denotes the fraction of incoming payments with which the household can abscond with if it defaults on its debts, off equilibrium. Assume $0 \le \gamma \le 1$, so (38) includes (18) as a special case. With this change, we then replace (26) with

$$-v'(n_t) + \mu_t - \gamma(1 + R_t^s)\lambda_t^2 = 0. \tag{39}$$

Then, following the same approach as for the original version of the model, in eliminating the multipliers using (22)–(25) and (39), we get (27) and

$$-v'(n_t) + \frac{(1 - \gamma)(1 + R_t^s)u'(c_t)}{(1 + R_t^f)} - +\beta\gamma(1 + R_t^s)u'(c_{t+1}) = 0. \tag{40}$$

Then, in a stationary symmetric equilibrium, from (40),

$$R^s = -1 + \frac{v'(c)}{u'(c)}\frac{1}{\beta\gamma} - \frac{(1 - \gamma)}{\beta\gamma\alpha}. \tag{41}$$

And, from (31)–(33),

$$c = \frac{\bar{b}}{1 - \frac{1-\gamma}{\alpha}}. \tag{42}$$

In (41) and (42), α denotes the central bank's implementation corridor, measured as

$$\alpha = \frac{1 + R^f}{1 + R^s}.$$

Then, from (29) and (30), the following must hold in equilibrium:

$$\alpha \ge 1 \tag{43}$$

$$R^s \le \frac{1}{\beta\alpha} - 1 \tag{44}$$

So, in equilibrium, the corridor α and fiscal policy $\bar{b}$ determine consumption c, from (42), and then the interest rate on reserves is determined by (41), given c and α.

So, from (41) and (42), a larger corridor α implies lower consumption c, and therefore lower welfare, given that welfare is proportional to

$$u(c) - v(c), \tag{45}$$

and $c < c^*$ in this equilibrium. As well, a larger corridor implies a higher interest rate on reserves. Since c decreases, therefore s must fall from (33). This effect is something like what happens in a Poole model, in that lower reserves imply a larger corridor, but this happens for an entirely different reason than in the Poole model. Here, a larger corridor tightens the household's collateral constraint, and in equilibrium this implies that a smaller quantity of reserves is needed to support a smaller quantity of retail payments. As well, in general equilibrium the interest rate on reserves must increase when α increases, whereas partial equilibrium experiments in the Poole model fix the interest rate on reserves.

If the quantity of safe assets increases, then from (42) consumption c increases, and welfare goes up as well. So, from (41) the interest rate on reserves increases. As well, from (33) reserve balances must increase to support more retail transactions. A larger quantity of safe assets is beneficial, as this relaxes the household's collateral constraint.

What is optimal monetary policy here, given fiscal policy $\bar{b}$? From (42), reducing α increases consumption, and welfare, from (45). So, from (43) if $\alpha = 1$ is a feasible policy, this is optimal. Given $\alpha = 1$, from (42) we have

$$c = \frac{\bar{b}}{\gamma},$$

and then, provided that the collateral constraint binds at the optimum, that is

$$\bar{b} < \gamma c^*,$$

then from (41) the interest rate on reserves at the optimum is

$$R^s = -1 + \frac{v'\left(\frac{\bar{b}}{\gamma}\right)}{u'\left(\frac{\bar{b}}{\gamma}\right)} \frac{1}{\beta\gamma} - \frac{(1-\gamma)}{\beta\gamma},$$

and it is easy to show that (44) holds at the optimum, as

$$\frac{v'\left(\frac{\bar{b}}{\gamma}\right)}{u'\left(\frac{\bar{b}}{\gamma}\right)} < 1.$$

So, as long as the collateral constraint binds at the optimum, that is safe assets are sufficiently scarce, then a floor system with $R^f = R^s$ is optimal. And, as in the Poole model, this implies that, beyond the quantity of reserves required to support transactions, $s = \frac{\bar{b}}{\gamma}$, the household is indifferent concerning how much reserves are held.

Note, however, that a floor system is optimal in the model purely for efficiency reasons. Basically, a floor system serves to relax collateral constraints. The conventional reasons given for floor systems are that they are necessary for quantitative easing, that they make monetary policy implementation easy, or that a large quantity of reserves somehow lubricates the wholesale payments system. None of these factors come into play here, which seems interesting.

2.6.5 Extensions

While the results here are intriguing, much is omitted that could make the approach more interesting. In particular:

1. The model could allow for aggregate shocks. It would be useful to determine the central bank's optimal response to such shocks, which would imply an optimal policy rule for the overnight interest rate.
2. Most retail payments systems allow for daylight overdrafts – borrowing by financial institutions from the central bank during the trading day to bridge the gap between outgoing and incoming payments. Incorporating this would involve either multiperiod clearing and settlement in the wholesale payments system or a continuous time approach.
3. In the model, households (banks) always hold overnight reserve balances. While it may be the case, as in the model, that the central bank's borrowing facility is little used in practice, for example in Canada, it would be useful to modify the setup so that reserve balances can go to zero overnight.

3 Quantitative Easing and Monetary Policy Implementation

This section draws in important ways from two pieces of work. The first is Williamson (2016), which is a particular theory of quantitative easing (QE) and how it works. The second is Williamson (2017), which evaluates the theoretical and empirical literature on QE.

Floor systems have sometimes evolved as an afterthought for central banks – a necessary feature if the central bank is engaged in QE. For example, when the Fed first engaged in large-scale asset purchases in late 2008, it was understood that this necessitated operating a floor system so that, under then current arrangements, the overnight nominal interest rate would be stuck at zero as long as the Fed maintained a large stock of reserves in the financial system. It was therefore decided that implementation of interest payments on reserves, which had been approved by Congress, would be moved up to October 2008, to allow the overnight rate to increase while the floor system was still in place, should the FOMC decide this was necessary.

Some early advocates considered a floor system and QE as an integrated whole, in that a large central bank balance sheet, it was argued, could have implications for monetary policy implementation. For example, Goodfriend (2002) argued, using a version of the Poole model, that a floor system would make monetary policy implementation much easier in the United States (see also Ennis and Weinberg 2022 for a later perspective on Goodfriend's views).

That is, as in the Poole model, pegging the overnight rate just amounts to administering the interest rate on reserve balances, in this view. Further, Goodfriend argued, the large central bank balance sheet would give the central bank an extra policy instrument – balance sheet policy – in addition to interest rate policy. Goodfriend's primary concern seemed to be with implementation – that a floor system would be easier to operate than a corridor system. In particular, according to Goodfriend's argument, operating a corridor system in the US context requires forecasting the demand for reserves on a particular day, then supplying the quantity of reserves that implies a market-clearing overnight interest rate as close to the target as possible. Further, the target interest rate in the Fed's corridor system was the fed funds rate, which cannot be observed in real time, as much of the federal funds market is over-the-counter. Intervention by the Fed takes place in the repo market, so in principle the Fed could have intervened by auctioning off funds at the target interest rate – much as the Fed's reverse repo facility works – but this was not how the Fed chose to do things. That is, given how the Fed conducted policy in its corridor system (not that this was necessarily optimal), a floor system could well have looked like a much simpler approach to monetary policy implementation in the United States.

Quantitative easing (QE) was implemented, mainly post-global financial crisis (2008–2009), by a number of central banks, including the Fed, the European Central Bank (ECB), the Swedish central bank, the Swiss National Bank, and the Bank of Japan. The simplest type of QE operation is a swap of reserve balances for long-maturity government debt. For example, the Bank of Canada's large-scale asset purchases during the COVID-19 pandemic were mainly of this type. However, some central banks have ventured into the practice of purchasing private assets. For example, the Fed has purchased mortgage-backed securities, the Bank of Japan has purchased exchange-traded funds, and the Swiss National Bank has purchased equity claims.

Central bankers typically show an interest in QE operations when the short-term nominal interest rate can go no lower or is as low as policymakers will tolerate. Some central banks – the Bank of Japan, the Swiss National Bank, and the European Central Bank, for example – have at times opted for a policy rate that is below zero. But the Fed treats a fed funds rate of zero as its lower bound, while the Bank of Canada has never targeted its policy rate lower than 0.25 percent. So, at the lower bound on the target nominal interest rate, a central banker may desire further monetary easing, and it has been argued that this can be achieved in this context with QE. Effectively, QE acts to shorten the average maturity of the consolidated government debt, which includes all the liabilities of the central bank and the central government. That is, reserve balances are overnight assets – as short a maturity as is possible – which are swapped in a QE operation for long-maturity assets. The average maturity of the central bank's asset portfolio then lengthens, while the average maturity of assets held in the private sector falls.

But why would QE matter? Effectively, QE is consolidated government debt management, and before central banks started engaging in QE, debt management was not considered a part of the policy stabilization toolkit. Central bankers have typically argued (e.g. Bernanke 2010, 2020) that QE works in part because of asset market segmentation. Different individuals or financial institutions have preferences for assets of particular maturities. Then, an asset swap by the central bank involving assets of different maturities changes the relative supplies of assets held by the public, and therefore, due to market segmentation, the relative prices of assets must change. For example, if the central bank buys long-maturity government bonds with reserve balances, then long bond yields should fall and the yield curve should flatten, according to the argument.

An effect of QE in general relies on central bank asset purchases not being undone by the private sector. That is, a policy neutrality theorem such as Wallace (1981) cannot hold. For example, the Fed may be able to turn long-maturity assets into short-maturity assets, but that is also the function of private sector financial intermediaries. Somehow, the central bank must be better at maturity transformation than is the private sector for QE to have an effect. And perhaps QE could work by constraining the central bank. For example, it is sometimes argued that QE could be effective through a signaling effect. That is, there may be a payoff to forward guidance – a commitment by the government to a future action, that it may choose not to take were it not able to commit. And, it is argued (e.g. Bhattarai et al. 2022), that structuring the central bank's asset portfolio through QE could give the central bank the required commitment.

To expand on this, there are essentially three approaches widely emphasized in the literature. These are:

1. *Portfolio Balance or Segmented Markets Theory.* When central bankers use QE, they appear to believe that purchases of long-maturity assets will make the yield curve flatter. That is, with short-term interest rates at zero, or close to it, declines in long-term interest rates will narrow the margin between long-term and short-term rates. In portfolio balance or segmented markets theory, assets with different characteristics are imperfect substitutes, and one dimension on which characteristics of assets differ is maturity. According to the theory, assets of different maturities are imperfect substitutes because of frictions that inhibit arbitrage across maturities – assets are costly to buy and

sell for example. Portfolio balance is the essence of older static theories of asset markets, for example Tobin (1969), which starts by assuming that there exist well-defined asset demand and supply functions for different assets. Then, in such a model, the central bank can affect the relative rates of return on assets by altering their relative supplies. The idea applies equally well to assets that are different according to maturity or according to some other characteristic.

2. *Preferred Habitat Theory.* This theory is closely related to portfolio balance theory and seems to have been articulated first by Modigliani and Sutch (1966). A modern technical version of the theory is in Vayanos and Vila (2021). The idea is that we can think of financial market participants as having preferences over maturities of assets. For example, life insurance companies have long-maturity liabilities, so to hedge risk these financial intermediaries have a preference for long-maturity assets – a preferred habitat in the long end of the term structure. Similar arguments apply to other types of financial intermediaries – banks, mutual funds, and so on. For the effects of QE, this leads to the same conclusions as portfolio balance theory. We could think of the key difference between portfolio balance theory and preferred habitat theory being that portfolio balance theory posits that relative supplies of assets matter because of frictions in asset market exchange, while in preferred habitat theory relative asset supplies matter because of underlying differences in preferences over assets.

3. *Signaling.* It is possible that QE does not have significant direct quantitative effects on interest rates, inflation, or aggregate economic activity. Indeed, there are theoretical results, for example Wallace (1981), which demonstrate that, even in economies with important financial frictions (e.g. limits on trade that generate a role for currency and/or government debt), central bank portfolio decisions can be irrelevant, if we take proper account of effects working through fiscal policy. Basically, these ideas work like the Modigliani–Miller theorem in corporate finance, except in this case the fiscal consequences of monetary policy actions undo the effects of those actions. But, even if there are no direct effects of QE, commitment to future monetary policy can matter for economic outcomes in the present, and QE may be a means for the central bank to commit. That is, the structure of the central bank's current asset portfolio may bind future monetary policy-makers to particular actions. Such arguments have been made by Woodford (2012) and Bhattarai et al. (2022).

In the next subsection, we will provide a specific example of how QE might work, related to Williamson (2016), which builds on a Lagos–Wright (2005) framework. The theory of QE embodied in this model is quite different from portfolio balance, preferred habitat, or signaling theories of QE. In our model, QE works because of an asymmetry between the private sector and the central bank. That is, private banks face an incentive problem. They have limited commitment, but this can be mitigated if banks back their deposit liabilities with safe assets. Effectively, this is collateralization, but the collateral is imperfect in that it can be diverted by the bank should the bank opt to default on its liabilities. Key to the QE effect is that long-maturity government debt can be diverted more easily than short-term government debt – implicitly, long-maturity debt receives a larger haircut than short-maturity debt, as observed in practice. But the central bank is assumed not to face any incentive problem – there are financial frictions in the private sector but not at the central bank. Then, in this context, the central bank can unload long-maturity debt from the private sector, replacing it with reserves – short-term debt. Provided that safe assets are in short supply in the aggregate, this increases the effective stock of collateral in the economy, relaxes banks' collateral constraints, flattens the yield curve, and increases welfare.

In terms of monetary policy implementation, the fact that the average maturity of the central bank's asset portfolio matters could change things. Certainly, QE implies that control of the overnight interest rate is different – there is a floor system rather than a corridor system. But, at the extreme, the central bank could care about the whole government yield curve, rather than just an overnight interest rate – yield curve control, effectively. Or, as is now standard practice, the central bank could express its intermediate targets in terms of an overnight interest rate and a rate of asset purchases per unit time.

3.1 A Model of QE

Time is indexed by $t = 0, 1, 2, 3, \ldots$, and each period has two subperiods, denoted the centralized market (CM) and decentralized market (DM). The population consists of a continuum of *buyers*, and a continuum of *sellers*, each with unit mass, along with a finite number of banks. Each buyer has preferences given by

$$E_0 \sum_{t=0}^{\infty} \beta^t [-H_t + u(x_t)],$$

where H_t denotes labor supply in the CM and x_t denotes consumption of the buyer during the DM. Assume that $0 < \beta < 1$, and that $u(\cdot)$ is a strictly increasing, twice continuously differentiable, and strictly concave utility function with $u(0) = 0$ and $u'(0) = \infty$. Further, $u(\hat{x}) - \hat{x} = 0$ for some $\hat{x} > 0$. Define x^* as the solution to $u'(x^*) = 1$. The quantity x^* will be important when we want to think about efficiency in this model. Each seller has preferences

$$E_0 \sum_{t=0}^{\infty} \beta^t [X_t - h_t],$$

where X_t is consumption in the *CM* and h_t is labor supply in the *DM*. Consumption goods can be produced one-for-one with labor input by the buyers in the *CM*, and by the sellers in the *DM*, and consumption goods are perishable.

Each bank has preferences given by

$$E_0 \sum_{t=0}^{\infty} \beta^t [X_t - H_t],$$

where X_t, and H_t, respectively, denote consumption and labor input for the bank. So, a bank is active only in the *CM*, where it can consume and can produce perishable consumption goods one-for-one with labor input.

All economic agents are present in the *CM*, but in the *DM* there is random matching between buyers and sellers. All economic agents are subjected to limited commitment in that they cannot be forced to work. Further, in the *DM* individual agents' histories are not observable. In a matched buyer/seller pair, the buyer wants to consume and cannot produce, while the seller can produce and does not want to consume. But, given the absence of observable history for the buyer, they cannot trade a personal IOU for goods. As well, buyers are not able to post collateral in a *DM* transaction and cannot trade government debt. However, they will be able to trade the liabilities of a third party – banks. Banks have limited commitment but possess a collateral technology permitting them to post government debt to back their deposit liabilities. But the collateral technology is limited in that the bank may be able to abscond with some collateral if it chooses to default. That is, the bank's assets will play the role of collateral but not in the legal sense as with a repurchase agreement contract, where the collateral is effectively locked up.

The consolidated government issues one-period government debt (short-term debt) and perpetuities (long-term debt). Short-term government debt consists of one-period nominal bonds, which each sell in period t for one unit of money, and pay off R_t units of money each in period $t + 1$, while long-term government debt is the stock of perpetuities issued by the government, selling in period t for q_t units of money, and paying off one unit of money forever. The consolidated government budget constraint is given by

$$\bar{c}_t + \bar{b}_t^s + q_t^l \bar{b}_t^l = \frac{\bar{c}_t + R_{t-1}\bar{b}_{t-1}^s + \bar{b}_{t-1}^l}{\pi_t} + q_t^l \frac{\bar{b}_{t-1}^l}{\pi_t} + \tau_t,$$

where $\bar{c}_t$ denotes the stock of currency in units of the *CM* good in period t, $\bar{b}_t^s$ is the real supply of short-term government debt, $\bar{b}_t^l$ is the real supply of long-term government debt, and τ_t is the lump sum transfer to each buyer in the *CM* in period t. Assume that bank reserves are equivalent to short-term government debt (we assume there is no transactions role for reserve balances), so $\bar{b}_t^s$ can be taken to include the stock of reserves. As well, the fiscal authority follows a particular rule. That is, the fiscal authority targets v_t, the real value of the consolidated government debt, in that

$$v_t = \bar{c}_t + \bar{b}_t^s + q_t^l \bar{b}_t^l. \tag{46}$$

This fiscal rule is a convenient way to separate fiscal policy from monetary policy in that the fiscal authority determines the real value of the consolidated government debt and then the central bank determines its composition. Given the nature of QE – a debt management policy conducted by the central bank rather than the fiscal authority – it seems clear that the interaction between monetary and fiscal policy could make a big difference for our results. But a general principle is that the effects of monetary policy – even conventional monetary policy – depend critically on fiscal policy. An extreme example of this is the fiscal theory of the price level (e.g. Cochrane 2023) and Wallace (1981) could be interpreted as implying that monetary policy only matters when fiscal policy is not held constant, in a well-defined sense. The bottom line is that assumption (46), while plausible, is not innocent. An alternative specification of fiscal policy could make important differences for the results.

3.1.1 Bank Behavior

We will assume that sellers of goods in the *DM* either accept currency or bank liabilities, but no one accepts both. The fraction accepting currency is ρ, and the fraction accepting bank liabilities is $1 - \rho$, where $0 < \rho < 1$. Thus in the *CM*, each buyer has probability ρ that they will need currency, and banks in part insure buyers against the need for currency in transactions. Assume that, in the *DM*, each buyer makes a take-it-or-leave-it offer to the seller.

In the *CM*, debts are first repaid, then buyers write deposit contracts with a bank, and there is asset market trade. At this stage buyers do not know what type of seller they will be matched with in the next *DM*, but they learn this at the end of the period, after consumption and production occur and after deposits with banks are made. At the end of the period, a buyer can only contact the bank with which they have a deposit contract, and a buyer cannot hold a deposit contract with more than one bank, by assumption.

A deposit contract consists of (k_t, c_t, d_t), where k_t is the quantity of goods – or the equivalent amount in assets – that an individual buyer must deposit with the bank, in exchange for the right to either withdraw c_t in currency at the end of the period or trade away d_t claims to period $t + 1$ consumption in the *DM*. The bank chooses the deposit contract (k_t, c_t, d_t), and its asset portfolio (b_t^s, b_t^l), where b_t^s is the real quantity of short-term government debt and b_t^l is the real quantity of long-term government debt.

So, in equilibrium a bank solves

$$\max_{k_t, c_t, d_t, b_t^s, b_t^l} \left\{ -k_t + \rho u \left(\frac{\beta c_t}{\pi_t} \right) + (1 - \rho) u \left(\beta d_t \right) \right\} \tag{47}$$

subject to

$$k_t - \rho c_t - b_t^s - q_t b_t^l + \beta \left[-(1 - \rho)d_t + \frac{R_t}{\pi_t} b_t^s + \left(\frac{1 + q_t^l}{\pi_t} \right) b_t^l \right] \geq 0, \tag{48}$$

$$-(1 - \rho)d_t + \frac{R_t(1 - \theta^s)}{\pi_t} b_t^s + \left(\frac{1 + q_t^l}{\pi_t} \right) (1 - \theta^l) b_t^l \geq 0. \tag{49}$$

In (47), the objective function is the expected utility of the bank depositor, who will make a take-it-or-leave-it offer to the seller they meet in the *DM*, with the seller accepting currency with probability ρ and accepting bank deposits in exchange with probability $1 - \rho$. Inequality (48) states that the bank's expected present-value payoff is nonnegative, and inequality (49) is the collateral constraint, which states that the bank prefers, in the next *CM*, to settle its deposit liabilities, rather than sacrificing collateral (short and long bonds). The parameters θ^i, for $i = s, l$, denote the fraction of the collateral asset that the bank can abscond with, should it default, off equilibrium. Assume that $\theta^s < \theta^l$. That is, if we think of θ^i playing the role of a haircut, the assumption that the bank can abscond with a larger fraction of the payoff and market value of long-term debt is consistent with the observation that haircuts tend to be larger on long-term than on short-term debt (see for example Williamson 2016).

The bank solves the problem (47) subject to (48) and (49) in equilibrium as, if it did not, then another bank could offer a deposit contract earning nonnegative expected present-value profits that makes depositors better off, and therefore takes away all the bank's depositors. Implicit in the problem is that the bank perfectly diversifies across a positive mass of depositors, exploiting the law of large numbers.

At this stage, we restrict attention to stationary equilibria in which fiscal and monetary policy are constant for all time, and all real endogenous variables are constant forever. Therefore, we will drop time subscripts in the analysis. At the optimum, (48) holds with equality. Then, let λ denote the multiplier associated with (49), x_1 the consumption of the depositor should they meet a seller who accepts currency and x_2 consumption if the depositor meets a seller accepting claims on a bank. The first order conditions for an optimum from the bank's problem, (47) subject to (48) and (49), are

$$-1 + \frac{\beta}{\pi} u'(x_1) = 0, \tag{50}$$

$$\beta \left[u'(x_2) - 1 \right] - \lambda = 0, \tag{51}$$

$$-1 + \frac{\beta R}{\pi} + \frac{\lambda R(1 - \theta^s)}{\pi} = 0, \tag{52}$$

$$-q^l + \frac{\beta(1 + q^l)}{\pi} + \left[\frac{(1 + q^l)(1 - \theta^l)}{\pi} \right] \lambda = 0. \tag{53}$$

Then, from (50)–(53), we obtain the following asset pricing relationships:

$$R = \frac{u'(x_1)}{[\theta^s + (1 - \theta^s)u'(x_2)]}, \tag{54}$$

$$q^l = \frac{\theta^l + (1 - \theta^l)u'(x_2)}{R\theta^s - \theta^l + u'(x_2) \left[R(1 - \theta^s) - 1 + \theta^l \right]}. \tag{55}$$

In (54) and (55), the quantities x_1 and x_2 are endogenous, but the two relationships (54) and (55) tell us something about how financial frictions affect asset prices. Specifically, $u'(x_1)$ reflects inefficiency in *DM* exchange where currency is used in transactions, while $u'(x_2)$ reflects a similar inefficiency in *DM* exchange involving claims on banks. The first inefficiency arises due to a conventional effect of anticipated inflation on transactions using zero-nominal-interest media of exchange (currency in this case). The second inefficiency arises because of a short supply of safe assets, reflected in a binding collateral constraint for banks. In general, the higher is the marginal utility of consumption in *DM* exchange, the lower is total surplus in exchange, and the greater is inefficiency.

Equation (54) states that the gross one-period nominal interest rate R must reflect relative inefficiencies in transactions involving currency and transactions involving claims on banks, as well as the fraction of short-maturity government debt that is subject to diversion by the bank. As well, the gross real rate of return on one-period government debt, from (50) and (54) is

$$\frac{R}{\pi} = \frac{1}{\beta [\theta^s + (1 - \theta^s)u'(x_2)]}, \tag{56}$$

which depends on the inefficiency in transactions involving bank claims and the ability of the bank to abscond with short-term government bonds.

From (55), the price of long-term government debt depends on R, the yield on short-term government debt, on θ^l and θ^s, and on the inefficiency in exchange of bank claims for goods in the *DM*. In particular, q^l decreases with θ^l, increases with θ^s, and increases with x_2, so bond prices are lower if long-maturity government bonds are less useful as collateral, higher if short-maturity bonds are less useful as collateral, and lower if inefficiency increases in *DM* exchange involving claims on banks. Perhaps more informatively, from (55) the gross yield to maturity on a long-term government bond is given by

$$R^l = \frac{R\left[\theta^s + (1 - \theta^s)u'(x_2)\right]}{\theta^l + (1 - \theta^l)u'(x_2)},$$

and the term premium is then

$$R^l - R = \frac{R(\theta^l - \theta^s)\left[u'(x_2) - 1\right]}{\theta^l + (1 - \theta^l)u'(x_2)}. \tag{57}$$

So, the term premium is greater than zero if and only if $\theta^l > \theta^s$ and $u'(x_2) > 1$, that is, if and only if long-term bonds are less useful than short-term government debt as collateral, and there exists inefficiency in the *DM* market where bank claims are traded. As well, the term premium is increasing in $\theta^l - \theta^s$ and decreasing in x_2, or increasing in *DM* inefficiency in the exchange of bank claims.

The next step is to solve for an equilibrium. Assuming the collateral constraint (49) binds (the quantity of consolidated government debt, v, is sufficiently small), substitute in (49) using (50)–(53) and the fiscal policy rule (46), assuming market-clearing in the *CM* for currency, short-maturity government debt, and long-maturity government debt, obtaining

$$v - \frac{(\theta^l - \theta^s)\, b^l}{(1 - \theta^s)\left\{R\theta^s - \theta^l + u'(x_2)\left[R(1 - \theta^s) - 1 + \theta^l\right]\right\}}$$
$$= \rho x_1 u'(x_1) + (1 - \rho) x_2 u'(x_2). \tag{58}$$

Then, a stationary equilibrium is a solution (x_1, x_2) to equations (54) and (58), given fiscal policy v, monetary policy R, and b^l determined jointly by the fiscal authority and the balance sheet policy of the central bank. Given our assumptions, there is a unique solution to (54) and (58), where (54) follows from asset pricing, while equation (58) is an equilibrium condition in the market for safe assets. That is, the left-hand side of (58) is the supply of safe assets. Note that the supply of safe assets is adjusted to account for the composition of the government debt. That is, the larger is $\theta^l - \theta^s$, and the larger is b^l, the lower is the effective stock of safe assets, everything else held constant. The first term on the right-hand side represents the demand for currency induced by the volume of transactions in the *DM*6 market. And the second term on the right-hand side represents the demand for short- and long-term government debt induced by the volume of transactions in the *DM* market that uses bank claims.

Next, working backward, given our solution for (x_1, x_2) we can solve for inflation and asset quantities. From (50) the inflation rate is given by

$$\pi = \beta u'(x_1) - 1. \tag{59}$$

The quantity of currency, in real terms, from (47) and (50), is

$$\rho c = \rho x_1 u'(x_1) \tag{60}$$

and, from (50), (55), and (60), the quantity of short-term government debt outstanding is

$$b^s = v - \rho x_1 u'(x_1) - \frac{\left[\theta^l + (1 - \theta^l)u'(x_2)\right]b^l}{R\theta^s - \theta^l + u'(x_2)\left[R(1 - \theta^s) - 1 + \theta^l\right]}. \tag{61}$$

So, the balance sheet of the central bank must adjust according to (60) and (61), given fiscal policy v and b^l, so as to support a particular interest rate policy R. This is important, and it is typically a step left out in New Keynesian analysis (e.g. Woodford 2003), where it is typically assumed that the central bank can dictate the short-term nominal interest rate. Essentially, equation (61) states that, given the gross nominal interest rate R, and the quantity of long-maturity government debt b^l not held by the central bank, the central bank issues reserves to purchase the required amount of long-maturity government debt and enough short-maturity debt that b^s is what remains for the private sector to hold, while satisfying the demand for currency (converted one-for-one from reserve balances) at market prices. In practice, central banks have control over only some administered interest rates (the interest rates on central bank loans and reserve balances for example), but some interest rates of concern cannot be dictated but depend on the size and composition of the central bank's balance sheet.

In analyzing policy, we can start with the effects of conventional monetary policy. Assuming that $\theta^l - \theta^s$ is sufficiently small, an increase in R, from (54) and (58), increases x_2 and reduces x_1. Then, from (59), inflation increases (a Fisher effect), but (56) implies that the real interest rate on short-term government debt increases. From (55), the price of long-maturity bonds falls, so the long bond yield rises. That is, there are two inefficiencies at play here – a standard Friedman-rule type inefficiency, according to which higher inflation reduces consumption in cash transactions, and a binding collateral constraint for banks, which is affected by the quantity of safe interest-bearing assets outstanding. From (60) the decline in x_1, associated with the first inefficiency, causes the quantity of currency, in real terms, to decline. And, from (61), the stock of short-maturity government debt increases, in real terms, and because the real stock of currency declines, the real value of total government debt (including long bonds) increases.

Next, we will model QE as a decrease in b^l, given fiscal policy v and conventional monetary policy R. From (54) and (58), this causes x_1 and x_2 to increase. Note that if we add utilities across economic agents in this environment, the resulting welfare measure is proportional to

$$W = \rho[u(x_1) - x_1] + (1 - \rho)[u(x_2) - x_2]. \tag{62}$$

Then, since $x_1 < x^*$ and $x_2 < x^*$ in equilibrium, where $u'(x^*) = 1$ determines x^*, which maximizes surplus in DM meetings, QE increases welfare. That is, long-maturity bonds are inefficient collateral, relative to short-maturity bonds, so reducing the quantity of long-term bonds outstanding increases the quality-adjusted stock of collateral, relaxing banks' collateral constraints. Further, from (57), the term premium declines, that is the yield curve becomes flatter. Finally, from (59), inflation falls.

This experiment in the model captures some of the features of QE alleged to exist by central bankers (see for example Bernanke 2010, 2020). In particular, the term premium falls and the yield curve flattens. However, in other ways the results seem inconsistent with how central bankers view QE. In particular, QE is typically characterized as an accommodative policy, which presumably should increase inflation, but inflation falls in this experiment. Also, note that b^l could fall as the result of fiscal policy and have exactly the same effect. That is, QE is basically debt management policy, conducted by the central bank. The central bank aims to have a beneficial effect by swapping short-maturity interest-bearing assets (reserves) for long-maturity interest-bearing assets. In the model, we can think of reserves as one-period nominal bonds which are equivalent to the short-term bonds issued by the fiscal authority. Further, while QE is typically characterized as an emergency policy, conducted in circumstances where conventional interest rate policy has reached a limit – the effective lower bound or some other lower bound dictated by specific policy concerns – the model says simply that the government should refrain from issuing long-term debt, as short-term debt is more useful in financial markets.

Note that, in general, the model says that a large-balance-sheet policy of the central bank is neutral, holding constant the maturity structure of the outstanding consolidated government debt. That is, a swap of reserves for one-period government debt has no effect on b^s and is irrelevant for all quantities and prices. Thus, while a case might be made for a large central bank balance sheet, in terms of monetary policy implementation and payments system efficiency, in general equilibrium there is no obvious benefit. Further, the conventional interest rate policy of the central bank works exactly the same in this model if there is a large central bank balance sheet with a floor system or a small central bank balance sheet with a corridor system. Changes in R, the gross nominal interest rate on short-term government debt, can be accomplished through open market operations, under a corridor system, or by administered changes in the interest rate on reserves, in a floor system, and the effects are identical.

If we take the model seriously, it tells us that there is more to monetary policy implementation than how a short-term nominal interest rate is targeted. In the model, the one-period gross nominal interest rate, R, matters for welfare, but so does the composition of the central bank's balance sheet, independent of R. So, the model asks us to go further in determining how the practical management of the central bank's portfolio should take place.

3.2 Discussion

This example only touches the surface in analyzing the effects of large-balance-sheet central banking policy. Other issues that arise are:

1. It would be interesting to study the reasons why long-maturity debt typically carries a larger haircut than short-maturity debt. To do this would likely require dealing with aggregate uncertainty so as to generate higher volatility in long-maturity bond prices relative to short-maturity bond prices.
2. Government debt management in practice, which could perhaps benefit from greater input from economists, is typically geared in part to satisfying the needs of financial markets. This seems to mean that financial institutions and investors have heterogeneous preferences for assets of different maturities. For example, financial institutions may prefer to match the maturity of their asset portfolio to the maturity of their liabilities. This is sometimes referred to as "preferred habitat," which has been studied by Vayanos and Vila (2021). But their work simply assumes assets-in-the-utility-function, and it would be interesting to explore why market segmentation can occur in environments where financial intermediaries are able to transform assets by maturity. Central bankers often appeal to market segmentation in explaining the effects of QE, but the key question is why the central bank is better equipped to transform assets by maturity than is the private sector.
3. The QE experiment in this section is the simplest, and most common, QE operation conducted in practice – a swap of reserve balances for long-maturity government debt, basically. But central banks have bought an array of assets. The Bank of Japan has purchased exchange-traded funds, the Swiss National Bank has purchased equities, and the Fed purchased a large

portfolio of mortgage-backed securities following the global financial crisis. The purchase of private securities by the central bank potentially affects the allocation of credit and opens up issues in political economy. That is, if the central bank is in the business of allocating credit, individuals and firms will have an interest in convincing the central bank to allocate credit in their favor. Williamson (2018) considers the effects of central bank purchases of private assets in a context where the quality of assets can be misrepresented at a cost.

4. The model here yields a quite stark implication for optimal government debt management. That is, since long-maturity government debt is bad collateral, the government should issue only short-maturity debt. Probably this should not be taken seriously, as alluded to in discussion point #2. In general, we need to know more about the roles of different types of government debt and how debt issue should be managed. As well, QE operations raise the issue of which part of the consolidated government – the central bank or the fiscal authority – should be managing the government debt. A consensus evolved in the 1980s and 1990s that inflation control is the province of the central bank. But could a central bank, given the right tools, do a better job of debt management than the fiscal authority?

3.3 Related Literature

There is a large literature on the empirical effects of quantitative easing, which includes Krishnamurthy and Vissing-Jorgensen (2011). A nice survey of the theory and empirical work is Bhattarai and Neely (2022). In terms of theory, Bhattarai et al. (2022) consider a model where QE has a signaling effect, and Gertler and Kiradi (2011) show how QE can matter if the private banking sector faces balance sheet constraints while the central bank does not. Williamson (2024) constructs a model in which QE matters for the efficiency of clearing and settlement in the wholesale payments system and the allocation of safe assets.

3.4 An Alternative Theory of QE

As the theory of QE appears to be incomplete, and few advances have been made recently, it may be helpful for the reader if we sketch out a potential avenue for research worth exploring. This sketch uses key ideas from the financial intermediation literature.

A central bank is a financial intermediary. It borrows from a large set of people – those who hold the central bank's primary liabilities, currency and reserves. And the central bank lends to the government, private financial institutions, and sometimes to private consumers (e.g. the Fed indirectly holds private mortgages which back the mortgage-backed securities in its portfolio). Like private financial intermediaries, central banks transform assets in terms of maturity, liquidity, risk, and rate of return. Therefore, the ability of a central bank to affect economic outcomes in a good way depends on it having an advantage relative to the private sector in intermediating assets. Perhaps surprisingly, none of the theories typically used by central bankers to justify QE – portfolio balance, preferred habitat, signaling – integrates financial intermediation into the analysis in a serious way.

To see how financial intermediation theory is important for understanding monetary policy, consider how conventional monetary policy works. The primary liabilities of a central bank are currency and reserves, which play important medium-of-exchange roles in retail transactions and in transactions among financial institutions. But we could imagine monetary systems in which the media of exchange used in transactions are the liabilities of private financial institutions, and those financial institutions create their own cooperative arrangements for executing transactions among themselves. Indeed, before the Fed, for example, opened its doors in 1914, much of the currency issued in the United States consisted of private bank notes. Those notes were issued by state-chartered banks during the free banking era (1837–1863) and by nationally chartered banks during the national banking era (1863–1913). From 1824 to 1858, one arrangement for interbank transactions was the Suffolk banking system, which operated in New England. Another example of a private monetary system was the pre-1935 note-issue system in Canada, under which chartered banks issued circulating notes and the Bank of Montreal (a private bank) acted as a quasi-central bank.

So, given historical precedent, the current functions of central banks could in principle be carried out by the private financial system. But there is a presumption that such an arrangement would be less efficient than having a central bank. Indeed, in the United States, it was decided in the early twentieth century that relying on private monetary arrangements is a bad idea. The argument, enshrined in the Federal Reserve Act of 1913, is that, in the absence of a central bank, the financial sector would be unstable and would be insufficiently responsive to fluctuations in the need for financial intermediation. The Fed was designed to stabilize the financial sector through discount window lending in crises and to accommodate the fluctuating needs for currency. Whether the framers of the Federal Reserve Act got it right is of course the subject of much debate.

In any case, the foundation for monetary policy rests on the central bank's uniqueness as a financial intermediary. In the case of the United States, in pre-financial crisis times the Fed's liabilities consisted mainly of currency and a relatively small quantity of reserves. Thus, the Fed was primarily transforming the debt of the US Treasury into currency. Given the Fed's monopoly on the supply of currency, and since private sector bank deposits are imperfect substitutes for currency, if the Fed conducted an open market operation – say a swap of reserves for Treasury bills – then this would matter. That is, through movements in market interest rates and portfolio adjustments by financial institutions and consumers, the new reserves created by the open market purchase would end up as currency. Thus, the Fed would have increased the quantity of intermediation it was doing, in nominal terms. Because this central bank financial intermediation was not offset by less private sector financial intermediation of the same type, there would be effects on asset prices, inflation, and aggregate economic activity.

But QE is fundamentally different from conventional open market operations. It is conducted in a financial environment in which there are excess reserves outstanding in the financial system. Given the interest rate on excess reserves (IOER), other interest rates and quantities adjust so that banks are willing to hold the reserves supplied by the central bank. It is generally recognized that a financial system flush with reserves, as has been the case in the United States since late 2008, is subject to a liquidity trap. That is, given IOER, which is set administratively, if the Fed simply swaps reserves for Treasury bills, then this may have no effect, because reserves and Treasury bills are roughly identical short-term assets. Indeed, such a swap may even have negative effects, as reserves may be inferior assets to Treasury bills. For example, at times the one-month T-bill rate has fallen below IOER, and the same has been true for Canada. For what reasons are reserves inferior to T-bills? Basically, reserves can be held only by a restricted set of financial institutions, while T-bills are more widely held and are useful as collateral in financial transactions (e.g. repurchase agreements) in ways that reserves are not.

When QE is conducted in a system flush with reserves the central bank is typically transforming long-maturity assets into short-maturity reserves. The key question, if we compare this to how conventional monetary policy works, is what advantage the central bank might be exploiting in conducting such a transformation. That is not clear. Consider, for example, a shadow bank (an unregulated financial institution that conducts bank-like activities) that holds long-maturity assets – Treasury bonds, for example – and finances its portfolio by rolling over overnight repurchase agreements (repos), with the Treasury bonds serving as collateral. This looks much like the asset transformation in QE, except it might actually be more efficient, as overnight repos may be superior assets to reserves, for the same reason that T-bills may be superior to reserves.

Therefore, from financial intermediation theory, it is not clear that QE should have any effect, and it might actually be detrimental to the efficiency of the financial system. Singh (2016) has made the case that QE has negative effects, due to the fact that it withdraws safe collateral from financial markets, thus clogging up the "financial plumbing."

3.5 Empirical Evidence on QE

The empirical work evaluating the effects of QE is summarized nicely in Bhattarai and Neely (2022). For the most part, QE empirical studies fall into one of three categories: (i) event studies; (ii) regression and VAR evidence; (iii) calibrated model simulations. The weight of the results is interpreted in Bhattarai and Neely (2022) as favoring the standard central banking narrative concerning QE. That is, according to the narrative, QE works much as conventional accommodative policy does – it lowers bond yields and increases spending, inflation, and aggregate output. But we should be skeptical of this interpretation. First, event studies look at the reaction of asset prices in a short window around a policy announcement. But the fact that asset market participants respond in the way that policymakers hope in response to a policy announcement with little historical precedent may say very little. Second, Bhattarai and Neely (2022) point out plenty of econometric problems in the studies they survey. Third, none of this empirical work actually measures the advantage that central banks might have in transforming assets when they conduct QE.

Primarily, we are interested in how QE matters for the ultimate goals of central banks – generally inflation and real economic activity. One type of empirical evidence we can appeal to is so-called natural experiments – instances where the policy was tried and the effects are more or less obvious. In Williamson (2017), two cases are examined: (i) QE in Japan post-2013 and (ii) Canada and the United States from 2010 to 2020. Since 2013, the Bank of Japan has had a 2 percent inflation target, but inflation was well below the 2 percent target from 2013 to late 2022 when, as in the rest of the world, inflation increased during the COVID-19 pandemic. Importantly, the increase in Japanese inflation during this episode was modest compared to most countries, peaking at about 4 percent. But the Bank of Japan was perhaps the first central bank to engage in QE, and QE operations in Japan were among the world's most aggressive after 2013. So, if QE is important in influencing inflation in the manner typically advertised, Japan should be a high-inflation country, not a low-inflation country.

Another example is Canada and the United States from 2010 to 2020. After the financial crisis in 2008–2009, the Fed went through three successive periods of aggressive QE operations, ending in 2014. Canada did not conduct QE during this period. However, the inflation experience in Canada and the US over this period, as well as labor market behavior, was much the same. Of course, this is not rigorous empirical evidence, but if QE were a powerful influence in terms of the ultimate goals of monetary policy, this should be obvious from the data.

3.6 Central Bank Independence and QE

Quantitative easing (QE) has the potential to threaten central bank independence, first through a mechanism involving maturity mismatch and second through the purchase of private assets. Maturity mismatch, as we have discussed, is an essential element of QE. The intention of QE is to shorten the average maturity of the outstanding consolidated government debt (total liabilities of the central government and the central bank), with the central bank increasing the average maturity of its assets and thus exposing it to maturity risk. Indeed, central banks with large balance sheets during the period of high inflation and monetary policy tightening beginning in 2021–2022 found themselves paying high interest on their liabilities (a large fraction of which were interest-bearing reserves) and receiving low returns on their asset portfolios, which were acquired when long bond yields were low. The result was a squeeze on central bank profits. It is potentially embarrassing, and a threat to central bank independence, if central banks actually lose money – which did not happen in the good old days when most of a typical central bank's liabilities consisted of zero-interest currency. And this is not only a perception problem, as QE is an attempt by the central bank to do debt management, and low central bank profits under QE reflects poor debt management. That is, the consolidated government could have saved on the costs of servicing the debt if the central bank had not conducted QE when interest rates were low.

The second issue for central bank independence of QE is the purchase of private assets. In some cases, central banks have attempted to keep private asset purchases at arm's length. For example, most of the Fed's private asset purchases in the period from 2009 to 2020 were mortgage-backed securities issued by US government-sponsored enterprises, backed by conforming mortgages – basically standardized mortgage loans. But, even if such arm's-length principles guide private asset purchases by the central bank, and more obviously if the central bank resorts to actions that potentially affect credit allocation, this opens the door to a breakdown in central bank independence. Central banks can come under pressure from interest groups, and the government, to favor particular sectors or establishments. For example, cryptocurrency enthusiasts have become powerful lobbyists, and central banks could come under pressure to purchase crypto assets.

4 Conclusion

This Element addressed issues in monetary policy implementation issues. The Poole (1968) model – the basis for much central banking analysis of implementation – was reviewed, and we studied its implications for monetary policy intervention, floor and corridor systems, and reserve tiering. We also studied a general equilibrium model of monetary policy implementation, which has some Poole-type features but corrects some of the problem with the Poole model by including retail payments, dynamics, and secured overnight credit.

Floor systems, which have become more prevalent in central banking since the global financial crisis, have potentially important implications for government debt management and the effects of conventional monetary policy. Quantitative easing (QE) has become an important monetary policy tool. So, we studied a general equilibrium model with banking, monetary policy, and fiscal policy, as an example to illustrate the potential implications for monetary policy. As well, issues were discussed relating to the modeling of QE, empirical work on QE, and the implications of QE for central bank independence.

Macroeconomic researchers have only touched the surface in this area of research, and much more needs to be done to deepen our understanding of monetary policy implementation. For example, more work is required in analyzing the relationship between secured and unsecured overnight markets, the design of wholesale payments systems, and the effects of unconventional monetary policies.

References

Afonso, G., Armenter, R., and Lester, B. 2019. "A Model of the Federal Funds Market: Yesterday, Today, and Tomorrow," *Review of Economic Dynamics* 33, 177–204.

Afonso, G., Giannone, D., La Spada, G., and Williams, J. 2024. *Scarce, Abundant, or Ample? A Time-Varying Model of the Reserve Demand Curve*, Federal Reserve Bank of New York staff report 1019.

Afonso, G., and Lagos, R. 2015a. "Trade Dynamics in the Market for Federal Funds," *Econometrica* 83, 263–313.

Afonso, G., and Lagos, R. 2015b. "The Over-the-Counter Theory of the Fed Funds Market: A Primer," *Journal of Money, Credit, and Banking* 47 (S2), 127–154.

Armenter, R., and Lester, B. 2017. "Excess Reserves and Monetary Policy Implementation," *Review of Economic Dynamics* 23, 212–235.

Baughman, G., and Carapella, F. 2022. "A Simple Model of Voluntary Reserve Targets with Tolerance Bands," *Journal of Money, Credit, and Banking* 55, 655–672.

Baughman, G., and Carapella, F. In press. "Interbank Trades: Why It's Good and How to Get It," *Journal of Political Economy Macroeconomics*.

Bech, M., and Garratt, R. 2003. "The Intraday Liquidity Management Game," *Journal of Economic Theory* 109, 198–219.

Berentsen, A., and Monnet, C. 2008. "Monetary Policy in a Channel System," *Journal of Monetary Economics* 55, 1067–1080.

Berentsen, A., van Buggenum, H., and Ruprecht, R. 2023. *On the Negatives of Negative Interest Rates*, Federal Reserve Board Discussion Series 2023–064. Washington, DC: Board of Governors of the Federal Reserve System.

Bernanke, B. 2020. "The New Tools of Monetary Policy: American Economic Association Presidential Address," Brookings Institution, Commentary, January 4.

Bernanke, B. 2010. "The Economic Outlook and Monetary Policy," Speech at the Federal Reserve Bank of Kansas City Economic Symposium, Jackson Hole, WY, August 27.

Bhattarai, S., Eggertsson, G., and Gafarov, B. 2022. "Time Consistency and Duration of Government Debt: A Model of Quantitative Easing," *Review of Economic Studies* 90, 1759–1799.

Bhattarai, S., and Neely, C. 2022. "An Analysis of the Literature on International Unconventional Monetary Policy," *Journal of Economic Literature* 60, 527–597.

Cochrane, J. 2023. *The Fiscal Theory of the Price Level*, Princeton University Press, Princeton, NJ.

Ennis, H., and Keister, T. 2008. "Understanding Monetary Policy Implementation," *Economic Quarterly* 94, 235–263.

Ennis, H., and Weinberg, J. 2013. "Over-the-Counter Loans, Adverse Selection, and Stigma in the Interbank Market," *Review of Economic Dynamics* 16, 601–616.

Ennis, H., and Weinberg, J. 2022. "Paying Interest on Reserves," in *Essays in Honor of Marvin Goodfriend: Economist and Central Banker*, edited by R. King and A. Wolman, Federal Reserve Bank of Richmond, Richmond, VA, 143–162.

Fuhrer, L., Juttner, M., Wrampelmeyer, J., and Zwicker, M. 2021. "Reserve Tiering and the Interbank Market," Swiss National Bank working papers, 17/2021.

Gertler, M., and Kiradi, P. 2011. "A Model of Unconventional Monetary Policy," *Journal of Monetary Economics* 58, 17–34.

Gertler, M., and Kiyotaki, N. 2011. "Financial Intermediation and Credit Policy in Business Cycle Analysis," in *Handbook of Monetary Economics*, Volume 3A, edited by B. Friedman and M. Woodford, Elsevier, Amsterdam, 567–599.

Goodfriend, M. 2002. "Interest on Reserves and Monetary Policy," *Federal Reserve Bank of New York Economic Policy Review* 8, 13–29.

Krishnamurthy, A., and Vissing-Jorgensen, A. 2011. "The Effects of Quantitative Easing on Interest Rates: Channels and Implications for Policy," *Brookings Papers on Economic Activity*, Fall, 215–265.

Lagos, R., and Navarro, G. 2023. "Monetary Policy Operations: Theory, Evidence, and Tools for Quantitative Analysis," National Bureau of Economic Research, working paper 31370.

Lagos, R., and Wright, R. 2005. "A Unified Framework for Monetary Theory and Policy Analysis," *Journal of Political Economy* 113, 463–484.

Lopez-Salido, D., and Vissing-Jorgensen, A. 2025. "Reserve Demand, Interest Rate Control, and Quantitative Tightening," working paper, Federal Reserve Board, working paper.

Lucas, R. 1980. "Equilibrium in a Pure Currency Economy," in *Models of Monetary Economies*, edited by John Kareken and Neil Wallace, Federal Reserve Bank of Mineapolis, Minneapolis, MN, 131–145.

Lucas, R. 1990. "Liquidity and Interest Rates," *Journal of Economic Theory* 50, 237–264.

Modigliani, F., and Sutch, R. 1966. "Innovations in Interest Rate Policy," *American Economic Review* 56, 178–197.

Poole, W. 1968. "Commercial Bank Reserve Management in a Stochastic Model: Implications for Monetary Policy," *Journal of Finance* 23, 769–791.

Shi, S. 1997. "A Divisible Model of Fiat Money," *Econometrica* 65, 75–102.

Singh, M. 2016. *Collateral and Financial Plumbing*, Second Edition, Risk Books, London.

Swiss National Bank. 2023. "Implementing Monetary Policy with Positive Interest Rates and a Large Balance Sheet: First Experiences," www .snb.ch/en/publications/communication/speeches/2023/ref_20231109_tmo.

Tobin, J. 1969. "A General Equilibrium Approach to Monetary Theory," *Journal of Money, Credit, and Banking* 1, 15–29.

Vayanos, D., and Vila, J. 2021. "A Preferred-Habitat Model of the Term Structure of Interest Rates," *Econometrica* 89, 77–112.

Wallace, N. 1981. "A Modigliani–Miller Theorem for Open Market Operations," *American Economic Review* 71, 267–274.

Williamson, S. 2016. "Scarce Collateral, the Term Premium, and Quantitative Easing," *Journal of Economic Theory* 164, 136–165.

Williamson, S. 2017. "Quantitative Easing: How Well Does This Tool Work?" *Regional Economist*, Federal Reserve Bank of St. Louis, Third Quarter., www.stlouisfed.org/publications/regional-economist/third-quarter-2017/quantitative-easing-how-well-does-this-tool-work.

Williamson, S. 2018. "Low Real Interest Rates, Collateral Misrepresentation, and Monetary Policy," *American Economic Journal: Macroeconomics* 10, 202–233.

Williamson, S. 2024. "Interest Rate Control and Interbank Markets," University of Western Ontario, working paper.

Woodford, M. 2003. *Interest and Prices*, Princeton University Press, Princeton, NJ.

Woodford, M. 2012. "Methods of Policy Accommodation at the Interest Rate Lower Bound," *Proceedings of the Jackson Hole Economic Policy Symposium*, Federal Reserve Bank of Kansas City, 185–288.

Cambridge Elements ≡

Money and Banking

Chao Gu
University of Missouri

Chao Gu has been Professor at the University of Missouri since she graduated from Cornell University with a PhD in Economics in 2007. Her research interests are macroeconomics and monetary economics. She has published in top journals such as Econometrica, Journal of Political Economy, Review of Economic Studies, Journal of Monetary Economics, Journal of Economic Theory, and more.

Joseph Haslag
Auburn University

Joseph Haslag is the Donald Street Professor and Department Head in the Department of Economics at Auburn University. Before his appointment at Auburn, Dr. Haslag served in the Economics Departments at University of Missouri-Columbia, Michigan State University, Southern Methodist University and as a researcher at the Federal Reserve Bank of Dallas. He has written extensively on macroeconomic and monetary topics.

About the Series

This Element series is an outlet for current research on money, banking, payment systems and monetary policy. Elements in the series will consist of a combination of literature reviews and frontier research.

Cambridge Elements ≡

Money and Banking

Elements in the Series

Monetary Policy Implementation
Stephen Williamson

A full series listing is available at: www.cambridge.org/EMAB

For EU product safety concerns, contact us at Calle de José Abascal, 56–1°, 28003 Madrid, Spain or eugpsr@cambridge.org.